## RELIGION

### GAEILGE

| | |
|---|---|
| Conversation | ✓ |
| Poetry/Rhymes | ✓ |
| Reading | ✓ |
| Written work | ✓ |

### ENGLISH

| | |
|---|---|
| Oral language | ✓ |
| Reading | ✓ |
| Written work | ✓ |

### MATHEMATICS

| | |
|---|---|
| Tables/Oral arithmetic | |
| Written work | |
| (a) computation | |
| (b) problems | |

### SOCIAL and ENVIRONMENTAL STUDIES

### ART and CRAFTS

| | |
|---|---|
| | ✓ |

### MUSIC

### PHYSICAL EDUCATION

### HANDWRITING

---

## Teacher's Report

...obert worked well this
...ear and I am pleased
...th his progress. Pleasant
...d co-operative at
...ll times.

Signed _Áine Ní Chuagáin CЯM..._
Teacher          Principal

---

## Personal Development

| | Ex | VG | G | F | See Report |
|---|---|---|---|---|---|
| ...ude to school | | ✓ | | | |
| ...rt to learn | | ✓ | | | |
| ...neral behaviour | | ✓ | | | |
| ...ngness to talk | | ✓ | | | |
| ...work – written | | | | | |
| ...homework | | ✓ | | | |
| ...ance | | | | | |

## *Also by Robert Kiely*

| | |
|---|---|
| *Gelpack Allegory* | (Veer, 2021) |
| *simmering of a declarative void* | (the87press, 2020) |
| *Some Sonnets* | (Earthbound Press, 2020) |
| *IN IT* | (Gang Press, 2019) |
| *How to Read* | (Crater Press, 2017) |
| *Killing the Cop in your Head* | (Sad Press, 2016) |
| *Fionn ag aislingeacht* | (Contraband, 2015) |

# ROB

*Robert Kiely*

ISBN: 978-1-915079-66-4

The author has asserted their right to be identified as the author of this Work in accordance with the Copyright, Designs and Patents Act 1988

Cover designed by Aaron Kent

Edited and typeset by Aaron Kent

Broken Sleep Books
Rhydwen
Talgarreg
Ceredigion
SA44 4HB

Broken Sleep Books
Fair View
St Georges Road
Cornwall
PL26 7YH

brokensleepbooks.com

# Contents

Area Studies                                        9

Acknowledgements                                    10

An Selected Poems                                   12

Chunk Identification                                13

Slug Leopard                                        14

Formula                                             15

Imaginary Subsumption                               16

Hair ft. Daniel Owusu                               17

Coin                                                18

This is Not Just an Elegy for a Schoolmate          19

Injections (A Play)                                 22

Biology                                             29

A Diagram                                           31

Gap                                                 33

Dissonance and Authenticity                         35

Love Poem                                           40

Plonk & Plaint                                      41

Long Winded                                         48

*for Nisha*

# ROB

Robert Kiely

But the educational system as it is can't but produce desperate gladiators.

…to sing those songs meant you shared something with the people who had sung them before.

## Area Studies

This is the greatest poem in the world.

I don't wanna hear one second more about "scenes"

who the fuck are you talking to where you

say it to my face

# Acknowledgements

Nisha Ramayya's *Notes on Sanskrit* doesn't have any translations in it, but it does have riffs. There are and aren't source texts. A language provides a surface. The whole pamphlet is about Sanskrit, about another language, yet not of or from it. In *The Language of the Gods in the World of Men*, Sheldon Pollock analyses Sanskrit as a vehicle of poetry and polity – a language, he suggests, best understood as a form of early statecraft. At the beginning of the Common Era, this sacred language was repurposed as a code for literary and political expression. At the beginning of the second millennium, local speech forms challenged and eventually replaced Sanskrit in both the literary and political arenas. Nisha's *Notes on Sanskrit* might seem humble, labelling itself 'Notes' on that language like some study-aid, but really it inscribes *on* it, deviating from it, spraypainting on it, desecrating it. We're all already woven into this, woven into this language which was and perhaps still is a tool for exercising power, to impress one's subjects and other polities and each other.
there are connections which you opt for
and ones you cannot opt out of
you know who you are
Looking through the telescope the wrong way, it just runs right off.
Falls off the tongue as an insult. We held hands at the entrance.
Teflon gates from tanks released. Nisha's poetry finds that Sanskrit has a surface which is manipulable, writes all over this non-dimensional point. It is held out as a certain length. Like Nisha's writing, Ziddy Ibn Sharam's *Acharnement* is a kind of graffiti, taking as its object contemporary literary culture in the U.K. right now, Arts Council funding applications, the Prevent strategy. That is the accretion Ziddy is confronted with and must alter by etching, chiselling, scrawling, spraying. I sometimes wonder if the politics we express in writing often cannot exceed the politics of its script, its typography, how we circulate it. *Acharnement* sidesteps all that. Ziddy and Nisha peripheralize themselves, lie down in the suburbs and banlieues of their something or other. But it is more than that: both of these pamphlets *grab* their objects, they find or make handles on them, they understand there's no going inside.

there's no singing in the shower
there's no singing in the streets
just because it sounds clear
    doesn't make it easy
  the only thing we hear
        is fatbergs, grease

There's this scar archive called music, a red smudgy stamp for repeating what your teacher tells you overand over. Leave the bibliographies to the scholars. Lemma, scythe ahoy. At the microscopic level, animals look all look the same: tubules with calcite crystals, a meshwork of divergent branching and rejoining. Subscription fees, the skeletons of ancient trees in timelapse explode, inside turns out. Sometimes I just try to hold on, when it confronts me as an object, like those songs which trip you up into the wrong beat pattern from the off sometimes out, taking the whole set to express and refuse all cuts, strumming the supply lines, holding it wrong. We're not getting to the bottom of it, we're inside and after it, and still making room for the sounds that are yet to come. Words like a broken clutch and every transmission a reception. Stingers spray across latitudes in potent glam, to smooth over the interval in tuning.

Nisha, Fred, Dom, Antonio, Frances, Nicky, Azad, Kashif, Cal, Bridget, Tom, Jack, Anouchka, Paul, Aaron, Sean, Jonny, Laurel, Luc, Emilia, Sophie, Alex, Naomi, James, Edmund, Daniel, Ian – errors and omisssions are collective just as genus is a wiki. I've given you each a letter or a note (do you remember?) and as you move around it changes the poem, depending on your definition of poetry. If you can't remember or lost it, don't worry, it's just like that sometimes. No need to reply. The chrysalis becomes wings and a half-life assert itself wholly, breaking then unbreaking rules of contact.

## An Selected Poems

If I was a submarine I'd wish I could fly.
These spoons are no good
but porous and dissolve in my tea.
You look confused.
Why don't you get out the kitchen
(my kitchen is outside).
And while we're on the subject, how many of ye here can say
I too am the spinach delving rod.
Don't throw up unless nonetheless wiser sideways goes drop
in the town of my enormous fluorescent upbringing
an ice-cap breaks free to fuck off.

## Chunk Identification

The life not lived sentimentally
justifies the one lived. Pulled by
ideas outside the close captioned frame
the lag equates the quality
and quantity of human life.
Even now the ghost
takes shape in the model of linguistic refraction
in which one thing
is mistaken for another – concise
and extractable like a modular component
or this or that universal socket,
where every distinction is but a fine point
on the physiological preconditions
of what we call reading the page,
the fine point infinitely small
shuddering in the branching clades.

## Slug Leopard

Some slugs think they are caterpillars. Some caterpillars think they are slugs.

Don't be so afraid of hurting others.

A dog sheds. A tree barks.

We align ourselves downstream, dreamily.

## *Formula*

it is a manager's credo

that sleep is not living

and so every night

we die because to live

is to be awake

# *Imaginary Subsumption*

The world is a network
of millions of teacups.

Some milky, some not,
some with a teabag.

This one is a fascist
thinktank. It has a storm in it.

This storm masquerades
as a storm of teacups,
even pretends to be a teapot.

And they all vibrate. They
all vibrate   in storm.

## Hair ft. Daniel Owusu

You cannot cut your own head off with your lungs.
        Scolded, small, feels like
stuck bronze. Fermented soldiers patrol the walls,
        folded into admiration. In the
cinema there's one person behind the screen, another
sitting, coughing. Every time they cough the one behind
the screen cringes up into a ball, like pancakes in a paper bag.

Our ears are shaped so intricately. Like roads, or pathways.
But really, our ears are hammocks, because sound travels and
so it needs a rest. This is community. Take the highest fevered
note of a dream, it starts off in the fingertips, discharges
to audio signals in electronics, stored in some server farm,
stored in wax, produced by bees. Hidden in pollen, later
unleashed from that into the localised slow-node, to re-start
some vibration in stilled fetid air, it creeps to reach slinking
into the ear, smashes its crystal, and sleeps.

Sentences are broken biscuits, compacted thickets.

Money is the last vestige of claws.

The diaries are chirping, antlers raw at the buffet. This pierce mingles
with managerial bequests. Pulling nostalgia from your teeth in chorus
to say yes, yes. Fuzzy roots mingling to bone.

How much money can fit in this room, and should we lie inside the hole,
its consecrated debt?

# Coin

Everybody's trying to cram as much world history into their poems
as they can these days.

Coins used to be cut from our hides then embossed.

Sometimes we write like every sentence is a gamble
that could throw the game.

In a flash the total destruction of all chance encounters.

There is exactly one point on the map at all times which coincides
with where it actually is right now.

It is cast better when a great cold is applied.

Dinosaurs were being dug up in Britain at the high point of its power,
so too with America and China.

Every coin is a warning.

Maybe the sample size is too small to get any purchase
on a wider spectrum.

We've all been in hiding for much too long.

# This is Not Just an Elegy for a Schoolmate

Stumbling down a main road
a death-threat inside an Ebeneezer
Howard or Geraldus Cambrensis
  effluent, cashed out to the middle-classes
   to avert the ills of socialism, all that
dribbled into your dead ear by a parish epidermis.

 People's experiences are different, but not that different from
   a cat in tenth-century Wales.
To determine its value its head was held down

its tail was held up and grain was poured over it
 until its tail was hidden, and the cat
was worth that much grain. Stop hitting

    yourself like the dopplering
of a field or a painted horse, I remember barely speaking to anyone
 and you screaming in French on cue always. 25 grains.

People either pull a whitey or have at it, so many
    casts hide evidence of something that might
  be self-harm but why talk about it.

 I remember my sudden death after a fight
with my father   and dying
  in a tunnel under a supernova  and knifed for a
   cigarette at the Carrigaline roundabout,
a kind of disgusting gelatin

buildup nearby in scaffolding, quivering and/or
  glistening, choose your own adventure,
    the whole thing not helped
  by that frog discovered skewered on the beak of

Barry Collins, which was at least a better option than what.
Broken arguments trundle on. Minds are wrecked then not,

get wrecked or not or the grotto bursts into
a shimmering five-dimensional
    barbed-wire, forming the text of whatever band
any number of people could have made it in. *Homeromastix.*
None of your experiences are yours anymore.
Counterfactuals stupefy, the wrecked is harder or the absence

of care for each other or giving into let's jump off that roof
    but never get skilled at it. 15 grains.
Balls caught on the gutter and all.
    I don't want to catch you I want to laugh at pain.

When I go back to where I come from and it is not Christmas
    no-one is there, all emigrated – those with degrees,
        largely to London,
            those with none to Australia or New Zealand

/ A recoil pours sauce on the sun. Standing with a tenner
in the interior of three regicides (which wouldn't be enough),
cruel laughs vent minute pandas into actions
    on another's behalf

drowning in grain then an inverted topography just to go halves on
    a nodge, which isn't at all like how everything baby animals do
is a further exaggeration of what is already happening. It's 30 grains
now, but the fifth attempt.
Are we the ground or the accountant? The cat was just one
    of many vague predicates in a moshpit, welcome

    inside the pearly gates of C. Harvey Rorke, 'An early
pricing model regarding the value of a cat:
A historical note,' *Accounting, Organizations
    and Society* 7.3 (1982), pp. 305-306.

Shame is our social relation. How could you have been
so still, in the growing pile.
    To be honest, I imagine it is already like
    no-one ever *really* knew you.

I'm a monster. Passion is for lice. Sentiment is a knife.
Sentiment is poppers
    round the carpark. Just strike the counter, growl again
and snap the band round the throat in something
which maybe is maybe isn't IS IT YET a heap.

*i.m. Paul Hodder*

# *Injections (A Play)*

- There are incursions of purgatory which fold interiors outside.
- The setting, the setting is clean and empty.
- They come and speak, junction boxes. Meat and mind intertwined.
- A set of circumstances removes habitual disease firebreaks, and we have been offered other firebreaks, firebreaks suspiciously similar to the way everything was already set up, no contact but contract.
- I will never put an untested chemical in *my* child.
- It is a kind of defeat.
- I will *never* put shit like that in my child.
- I am your child.
- Look you can put anything you want in *your* child, or the part I lay no claim to, as grandparent, like the foot or something.
- I am your grandchild.
- Will you pass that?
- No.
- The water has been turned off for an hour, I wish I filled some pans.
- Imagine there was a stream nearby.
- A stream.
- Or the sea.
- Shall we meet up?
- I'm not sure.
- I'd never put my children through that.
- I need some more time, I have to pick up the little one.
- I'm the little one.
- I have this voucher. I have this tip. Take them. Passes then to who.
- Perhaps a ritual would help?
- Help what?
- To avoid the chemicals.
- The music builds, speeds up. The houseplants grow chew marks indiscriminately. I am a visiting electrician, I enter with no tools, no, I do not enter. I knock. Knock knock.
- If we were near the sea, my autonomic nerves would get some rest, some fine tuning.

- But we aren't.
- No.
- Where does the water, the electricity, come from?
- I don't know. I'm still outside.
- The electrician is still outside.
- He comes in.
- Panting. The socket, it isn't working.
- A thousand years pass.
- Just because you say it, doesn't make it true.
- Such that the asparagus gets stripey-peeled, and served to our guests.
- Are you busy? 5 min. call?
- Finishes fixing it. There we go!
- Brilliant! I'd trust you with my life. Once there's no chemicals involved.
- Transforms into a deadline.
- Inexpressible shock and horror. L-look, please. I want to study and I am studying but also working and caring for my elderly grandmother. Please. I know I can get a good grade just with another 2 week extension.
- I will return.
- Many fathoms, many baskets woven in the sun. Fruit crates, their pliable warping, the simplicity of their stripes. In one week hobo chic.
- If this goes on, the insane double level in which I function, experience and recording, never able to commit and fulfil a purpose of either one-
- I've fallen out of bed! Please! My hip is broken!
- Helps them back into bed. ⎫
- Helps them back into bed. ⎬
- Helps them back into bed. ⎭
- Restitution mere pauper sauce. Release the cleats on these blind. Suction cups but less refined.
- The deadline returns.
- In a resigned voice. Look, please. I want to study and I'm studying but also working and caring for my elderly grandmother. She fell out of bed recently. Resignedly. Please. I know I can get a good grade with just another extension.
- I will return. What will change?
- Maybe everything.

- There will be others like me.
- What's your point? Just give up now?
- Shrugs. Maybe.
- Are these appeals nothing? There's inner forces at work here, its not usually only us here looking after such and such and so on, plus generations of particularly coded social formations and minor inheritances, of money and psychological problems big and small.
- The grade won't fix that.
- What will fix it? If I have more time perhaps I can offset it.
- The things you describe aren't here, they're on the stage, out there. Oort's cloud, 20 kinds of ice, impersonal forces of segmentation and deprivation, habits, jinxes, the whole gamut of neo-natal blurs, the wind-ups and wind-downs of cerebral climatology, the *actual* particles in the air, the shifts in taste and blame, the silence which only exists at absolute zero.
- I wouldn't put *any* type of ice in *my* child.
- What's this to me? I can only see you, not those inheritances you mention.
- Repetition, precision. It snows outside. It is snowing outside. Holds them, then them, in tender embrace. It feels too much sometimes.
- If your internet speed or computer processor speed is slower, you won't catch the good bits. Lag. Or maybe that's just the conveyor belt going in and out of simile prison, it all takes place in a ditch with a flying column, it all takes place at a moment when the passage of a planet reduces the brightness of that star, that's the deadline, the drama is in the levels of core, mantle and crust, its throwaway secrecy.
- There are things that I think-
- There are things that I think which I tell no-one, axioms by which I act, which I tell no-one, I cannot tell anyone for fear of being disabused.
- There are things I think too, separate things or perhaps the same, sentences through which thought becomes action and vice versa, which I do not tell anyone, for fear they are not true.
- And there are things I think, statements at my core, which shift to the mantle, which I tell no-one, for fear of being abused.
- And there are things I thought before, and still, and will continue to, which I have shared, which are not true, which I have shared and do not share anymore, and will tell no-one, anymore.

- The whole plane is tilted around us, so that from one of the localized uneven developments the higher plants appear to all share a similar physiognomy. Chewed.
- The pivot.
- Lines of altitude are not lines of solidarity, we enter certain social bodies.
- Not now.
- Indeed, and exit.
- Those bodies have legal personhood, but not with regards to entry and exit, the claim-
- Where is the new social body?
- It was stolen, and it might even have been a church.
- I'm out.
- The states, constrained to valleys and plains. Eleven developed stints in lived platitudes.
- Only liars complain, only local sentries, the starlings as friends sustain us, we are paired. They hold hands to deal with the risk of subsidence, when it is submerged, when it is submerged at last we will give it a new lick of paint.
- Tenant's broker, I just need a simple utterance, like, to get in the door.
- I'm so sad at home. I just want some control over how I work?
- Would you like to change teams?
- No.
- Alright, but I'm not sure what else would help.
- Why are there no scenes?
- They imply a changed situation or setting.
- And distract if not.
- The wholly active puppeteers the virtual, which puppets a smaller actual patch of light, etc.
- There is an utterance I hold inside in latent interior, filled with jargon, which I will soon share, which I hope will be useful, in time, or be our private noose.
- There's a knock.
- Knock knock. Knock knock. I'm the deadline.
- Lets them in. Look, I'm still catching up.
- Do you have any evidence?

- Repeats previous explanation, with a bit less emotion.
- Repeats previous encouragement, with a few terminological changes.
- Where have you been, while you were gone?
- I've been here the whole time.
- Pause. I wish you would actually leave. I love you but I wish you would leave.
- I know.
- Pause.
- Knowing is irrelevant.
- Pause.
- I know. I know.
- The deadline leaves. They don't tell you that you'll love, and will be loved in return, and will not be together.
- What I don't understand is the choice of coefficients which are chosen to be this or that to get an outcome we want. What do they actually describe?
- The erasure of stars.
- It hardly matters, now. That she's dead. The hips breaking.
- She had a fundamental niche.
- They hug. Let's go outside, let's bury her. I can't stand it, knowing she's in there. Indicates the room.
- What section of the garden? The tundra, the thorn scrub?
- ...the grassland, the karsk?
- Their advantages and constraints.
- Oh just fucking pick will you. I can't stand it, she's just in there. I can't. Runs out.
- OK. Grabs a shovel. Let's get started.
- They all go out.
- The garden. Tundra scaled down. If I step over here, I am in this terrain, if I step over here, another.
- The digging is finished.
- Yeah.
- There is mumbling. What's that?
- Neighbours, I suppose?
- The deadline wouldn't do that to us I suppose now would it?
- It could be any one of us! They laugh.
- I'll be needing some evidence of the death.

- Oh for sure.
- Like some kind of coin. All of them little deaths. The human grease stolen from Andean peasants.
- Shhhh. I want to hear the neighbours. All are silent.
- Pause.
- Mumbling.
- Even though there are more characters, no-one has entered.
- We have been right here the whole time.
- They've gone silent.
- They're listening for us maybe.
- Yes.
- Next scene. It is the garden still. Characters are gathering to reminisce.
- She was a bit difficult at times.
- We didn't always agree.
- But that's all water under all those kinds of ice.
- Yes. We mourn.
- Though we don't know how.
- There is no problem with losing. Pause. They don't tell you that you will lose, and lose again, and that each time the best part of you will be taken. They don't tell you that your own criteria will decompose. It's never enough, chewing the choicest cut of disgust.
- Pause.
- I remember the defeat of the American Century, of free movement, the defeat of hope, its falsely verdant balustrades, and I remember the defeat of the Etruscans, the losses so great their negative space does not matter, the defeat of honesty, the defeat of defeat, the replacement of supply chains by riots, the seemingly swift defeat of the gas station toilets and the box rooms, the defeat of yes brutal charm, the culpability and implications of it, and I remember their voices in my head, the defeat of the credit unions, the defeat of landlords the defeat of speculation, the defeat of property the defeat of victory, the defeat of public services the defeat of becoming a socialized, bourgeois individual and a cartographic attribution of agency booming the packaging more excessive than usual. The defeat of being too tired from work to be able to think about the aeons of nameless accomplice dead, who become antimatter, joining

them, executions with entrails pulled through nostrils, it was real, the defeat of that famed ambush, the execution of those terrorists, the waning of the sunlight. Pause. I can't wait to mourn all of this, I can't wait to mourn all of this, with all of you.

- Pause.
- Another pause.
- And another.
- Looks around. At the soil. I can't think like that. Quietly angry. Can't we think of a win. Calmly. I feel like I'm winning. Defiant. Winning all the time mate.
- Laughter.
- Tears.
- Every victory, no matter how miniscule, comes shrink-wrapped in a vicious court injunction against its very naming as such. Revisions to every meaning. Non-disclosure.
- I like this.
- I don't.
- Slowly, as if by osmosis, things turn, as in a rectilinear projection, they turn from the perspective not of a point or a line but a higher dimensional simplex. Complete. This person is now torn at by the others, some out of anger, some desperately seeking some of that feeling. They're killed dead, but not violently.
- Oh dear.
- Erm.
- Pause.
- Well, look, it happens, right?
- True.
- Lifts the arm and lets it fall.
- What now?
- I want a piece of them.
- I wanted to never be like that.
- A pause. Can we do both?
- Well. They chop the arm off. Let's inject it.
- The best bits of us, taken.
- We'll be renewed, and go out to lose it all again.
- The new contracts are in effect.
- You as you always were, on the back foot.

# *Biology*

The spandrel is not a scandal
but a middle metacarpal.
Start with something
historically specific
located in the air
and unlike most things spreads gradually
to the extremities. Everything either disappears or becomes rock
and gets lost in archival missive, that is its tempo,
the pure democracy of meta and counter veto.
Story is sound's afterthought.
The whale song accrues diphthongs, even
though there should be no animal noises
in poetry while they are in
abeyance outside.

\*

well we lie /// in wait or face
to suck on the edge of a cliff
   days of no diary. Look at the birds.
Soothe them with names. Names
never heard.


Each feather is asymmetrical like an object
across the waking boundary,
twirls, to be leitmotif.

\*

29

Pass the Ordovician to get a mouth
no qualia, qualified, then digital drips
rescind this bootlick quantified
in the slide from red
to yellow, declining equilibrium.
The viewing numbers too
parapet all kimono dulcet.
This is not about you.
A strand frees, the employees all crying in pure
empathic harmony, consoled
by their supervisors. Still managers.
If only we were telepathically linked
to ourselves. But it all
gets pushed back into the
new collective amnesia,
numbness is functional. You
know this it is all wrong.
Calculate the collective force
it takes to not break down
every day compound it.
Chartered emergence is bird-blur getting chewed up.

*

Laughter. To coo is that a nerve.

The thing's deformations sing.

# A Diagram

to mourn   is kettled
and every blow is shown
every blow is filmed close up
and beamed into our eyes
to show that endless misery
is truth not thetic trial
"the protestors turned violent"
is what some people *actually* say
they vote for increased police powers
they up their fucking pay
they pour money into shields
and bullets that crush bone
they pour it into selfies w/ corpses
on simple fucker's phones
they pour it into teargas
they pour it into batons
they pour it round like kerosene
and meanwhile they intone:

> "If only you'd stop screaming
> we could have a dialogue.
> If you'd do just what I say
> I'd have reason not to flog.
> If you'd eat the shit
> into which I spit
> I'd love you every day.
> If you'd not hurt
> you'd see what sport
> my way of life is today."

*

we watch, which is to say practice unceasingly
the re-ordering of the senses so that by night
we are in alignment. like each material act
is expenditure, stupid like an accumulation of
anything at all but loss re-aligned and continued
every day spat out so bad we can't even look
our loved ones in the eye. Take me to the gun
range, tied up or armed  take me to the gun range
    like feelings matter

\*


it's a given we bring in the local from
childhood as real as the local right now
an agglutination of trajectories, a sheaf
of neighbourhoods
some people's defence was to grow more quickly
just trying to get out
it is difficult to trust each other
with all the hissing
in those liminal spaces like hedgerows or after hours
building sites and the odd security guard
surrounded
it is a simple obvious circuit
with a recently replaced fuse

# *Gap*

If syllables are a weird subsection of music, which is an odd subsection of heat, then these things we call words are insane subdivisions rather than composites of syllables. In the movies they dodge the weapon in slow-mo just in time just as just in time production starts. Let that last bit be true. There then exists such antipodal points that the function of the sound is its derivative and its intervals are uncountable.

\*

cuts of composition, cuts of feeling removed from each other, cuts of cutting across one another in walking and talking, which are attempts at disintegration. cuts to funding, cuts of border in earth itself, the cuts on those rubber trees, the cuts the handout makes in the frame of the "artwork" to open it out to us. cuts water makes as it erodes valleys, the cut of hearing another sound from another room while listening to another again, the film feeling cutting or cut off, does it cut us

\*

    James & Nisha

light produces light but we isolate

all the extinct carbon based life of the earth and living

exhumed

can the extinct not rest

        exhausted

obviously, music is not a thing

but an absence    the gravity sink w/ a horizon

fall into the music

its soft hair   fractal tendrils preserve and encode

everything inside      everything that has been destroyed

there is no need to prove it

because it is not a proposition

# *Dissonance and Authenticity*

We were at the bottom of the stairs. I might have been anything between 8 and 11. I reached for your hand, but you refused it, since, you said, I was soon to be a man. The wallpaper kept changing. We haven't held hands since. I rewrite this later, wondering what age provides least embarrassment to me and what would be least for you. Maybe they coincide. It isn't happy, and it isn't sad. At the back of class in Ireland has been and continues to be deeply tied up with the British economy because those economies are intertwined. Class is an ordering and re-ordering of the world. In every generation classes are re-formed, re-made, old modes re-packaged, new entrants welcomed and former powers lost or shirked off. If we stereographically project the 4-dimensional knot of classes from the lumpenproletariat up to the ruling onto our 3-dimensional present, then further onto this 2-dimensional page hovering above it all, the lumpen would surround infinitely, the ruling classes, the 1%, tiny. When it rolls, that projection changes but it is still the same knot. A boomer moves from manual labourer to foreman, continues to socialize easily with labourers, is red-faced and deferential to the architects, earns more than his daughter can ever hope to earn, in fact continues to with that pension. Transformations occur, I mean there are 20 types of ice in the galaxy. If you gain access to the means of describing your situation that doesn't mean but not of it inside some economic determinism, fatalism, smearing could not but across the windscreens of a thousand BMVs but not of it, in transit between lascars and navvies and royals

> or in a pedagogy mourning a loss but not of it
> nobody here will lay a hand on you
> sure I've done some bad things probably
> now that I speak things come back slowly
> the weight of those hands
> the dappling of the light on the smooth wall
> it isn't smooth at all

Fathers. I hate them and must impress them
This is why I will repeat the same behaviour.
no pedestals, what is the family relation
after antagonism and aunthood, no pedestals

just a constantly shifting modality of a person's property held with their attributes, a sequence of transformations the aftermath of which we take to be class which used to be the older notion of fate or character, not just upward and downward trajectories, but the relative trajectories of alleged class positions and their subsequent impositions on others. Class is where people are at and how they talk to you bundled up with where they've been and where they're going, it doesn't help an upward trajectory which could not but in fact be *inside* a trajectory you will never exceed, sent to University or studying, writing assumed to be middle class even if about small bubbles components forced down as house prices rise almost sevenfold and access to the middle class via dating and here the writing which makes you more middle class and more poor with each letter you type and word you write or Curriculum Vitae what lifts away from the bubbles the roots they are somewhere the writing pulling you away you're not very grounded are you crushed down it isn't a good enough application for interview and can't get you up

what is the topology of that on the stairs

and you stand on the top and scatter the student papers down, and those near the bottom step well they stay there and those at the fifth step well they stay there but they're not of it and those at the top could not but not be of it. "There isn't a bomb in your bag is there?" the administrator in the Royal Opera House asks. My collaborator looks shocked. The walls new shades of tope. My father and mother grew up with many siblings, and when food was served it was chaos. For my father, if he didn't get to the food quickly, it just wouldn't be there. So he adapted – he ate quickly. In later life the fast eating continued. I was the eldest child with only two siblings. Because my parents ate quickly, I ate quickly, though the practical reason for the behaviour was gone. My fast eating is a kind of spandrel of their particular childhood experiences – experiences marked by class, or but not of it. It isn't sad, it isn't happy. Halfway up or down the stairs, the orientation is impossible to tell, the stairs which used to be a wheel of fortune, it must be up insofar as the bills and without a theory the house prices can only go up. What some people call an explosion is often just a mild loosening or tightening of the knot. Authenticity's bad essentialism. Could not but celebrate with a trip to the zoo. When you were a child you were asked if you wrote that yourself – this was the highest compliment. They could not but be complaining that students are being forced to make economic decisions about study, while lamenting that only one out of however many PhD students will get a full-time academic job. The only thing more provincial than provincialism is the critique of provincialism, you can extrapolate on from that. Here's another theory dropped as some change in Pat Tieney's poet's pot wrapped in a keffiyeh scarf. All of you write so simultaneously egotistical and passive; I'm being told I'm amphibian. Frogs of the world and all that. Erudite is taunt. Unskilled, like automatic, obscures technical know-how after the dignity of a hard day's work

Ratted out.

Did you draw this?

It's disgusting. I don't want to fight with a theory

of parvenues drifting around North America or Southeast Asia

this bit of paper demands that I die

in as slow a manner as medical science

can make possible with the moon on my back

holding my soiled underpants over my head

under the threat of slaps

            leather straps.

Grateful for the exposure.

The bell curve must be applied because the bell curve exists. It isn't sad or happy or even frustrating but we're sitting on our hands squirming. Did you write this? Authority distinguishes talent and effort, which distinguishes what I mean when I say "savage" from what you hear. For some time a major concept of natural history was the *scala naturae* or Great Chain of Being, an arrangement of minerals, vegetables, more primitive forms of animals, and more complex life forms on a linear scale of supposedly increasing perfection, culminating not in our species, whatever that could be, but our rulers. Some exams are held in a faculty. All the academics set an exam one question at least for many exams, let's say 100 modules. There are about 3,000 students, and each student takes 6 modules. Cooking always changes. The same pile of peas will taste different cooked on different days as their innate sugars become starches. Pastry chefs, hired for their cold hands, flicker in and out of existence. 18,000 separate exam papers. The exams are then split. Each exam involves answering three separate questions, which must go to three different markers. 54,000 pieces of paper, flitting between people. The wallpaper keeps changing colour. Security guards everywhere, watching things on their phones. Papers haunt our relationship to a body and space and time and not of it. Half of those must be second-marked, so 27,000 get spun around the system once more to another marker. Every day I make a marksheet, leaving it open and vulnerable to critique. Merit is a means of imposing scarcity on plenitude, stupid in a stupid poem of compulsive patterning but not of it, insistent like a lozenge in a pilot boat or could not but be drilling a pilot hole in the most brutal and sensitive of places – the bailiffs of literary criticism embalming what's caught in the throat in total comfort reaching out for assurance just a hand just something like the feedback inside static hiss. In photographs as you grow you move to the back, simultaneously lower on the steps and forward, but you know the eldest gets the land the next one goes to the priesthood and so on and so forth.

thinking around the drips,

Raised for slaughter we huddle inside words like tents

words like growth decline development evolution decay started as servants but ascending that stairs in a system of pure merit became masters, everything is read through historical inevitability, and we're still fucked even if we climb out of that.

It is as cold inside as outside

colder even, and when we get outside epigenetics hits

and I remember being told who fucked my mother

and when and what way complete strangers and I remember

telling them similar things, all of us

fucking each other's mothers, that was socializing

when it is a heart stent or a little tear with an inclination to obstruction. Pretty soon all our organs, such as mouthwash and toothpaste, will be considered vestigial. You know by who. People learn off the illegible by rote all the time. If my eye droops in sympathy with someone else's, whose nervous system is it really? The fusion of organic wealth and metallic fertility. The ending totally pre-emptive like an equation with a minus of a certain order of infinity at the end undoing what you're trying to work out. Futile doesn't get at it. The bottom drops out but not of it, nothing at all. You could not but give people access to the relevant spreadsheet but it might annihilate their valid working-out, is another mode of belly-flop. The bottom drops out of the organograms of our astringent benefactors, you'll feel a tightening of your tonsure even if you don't have one. The bottom drops out to accommodate longer than the bucket's capacity

it is something tender in me broken.

The bottom falls off, nothing at all.

It gets pushed down, the weight increases grows and grows

beyond its structural integrity the bottom drops out.

you've done some bad things

what does that word hold for you
you're moved to the front of the class
Some people wanted the cool experimental hand extended to them subjects of
lesser dents. Does my geographical location right now put me in an extractive
relation to that history? I came here to write. Which is fucked. Everywhere
people expect the work to get put in, maybe more so outside the alleged centre.
Going everywhere and everyone is cold, everywhere we go we have to earn,
anew each moment in the Americanized ruckus. If I'm not being read back
home then I'm not in a feedback loop, giving back, if I am the dominance
of the centre continues, and what happens to love when it gets tangled up in
the need for alternation, tied up with all kinds of denigration. The deepening
contrapuntal flow, its flute. The whole thing's not fraying at the edges, that's the
view from the core could not but yeah the edges to which they ship arms to to
stay core yeah the cloth itself woven of this fraying, a perfusion we have to eat, it
is toxic to us and them to everything we eat they eat it we eat it and puke it up
and eat it again to keep it down they eat it we eat it to see who'll last.

## Love Poem

the greatest poem is waking up in the same bed
            – in the gap between synchronicity and curation
    a shadow biosphere
encapsulates our hair

you pass through so many of me
and you, the angle of incidence as the object hits allegory
refracted to the listener

the moon is orange through measurable pressure
torqued to truth from us to a tube

the only way to write a love poem is too many drafts
and versions, don't make me write just one.
it could be anything, anything with you

# Plonk & Plaint

Study must be honest about the conditions in which it happens. In early 2020 I was invited to write "an additional piece on Irish poetry to balance the books a little bit" for an academic journal, which is commendable. I'd rather not so much have been contributing to a balancing of the books as attempting to unthink or at least unsettle certain distinctions or categories upon which those books are based. The labels on the ledgers. A distinction between British and Irish poetry, or between UK and Irish poetry. Though the aim of attempting to proportionately represent both sides of the copula is good (even if I often find in using both terms, the "Irish" side is *de facto* under-represented) it might need to be unsettled more. Many of the contributors to the volume in question would no doubt agree. Let's not speak of Irish and British poetry anymore. It might be better to speak of the Anglophone poetry of the Northeast-Atlantic archipelago, covering poetry of various languages and dialects from the Blaskets to Orkney and Jersey. It's a facet of what Ed Dorn called the North Atlantic turbine, whose centre is no metropole whatsoever. And even then, what gets externalized? In order to unsettle categories like "Irish," I initially wanted to demonstrate how they are unsettled in the poetry I read, I wanted to talk about distinctions between first and second nature, where roughly first nature would be the realm of objects or perhaps things-in-themselves, and second nature of accidents, perceptions, culture. Nature and history. Of course, these are straw figurines. Anyway, I wanted to make explicit a leyline of critical thinking in the poetry of Laurel Uziell, Frances Kruk, and Maggie O'Sullivan – poetry I've learned a lot from. I ended up writing a different essay.

National categorizations are knotted up with gender and class and other market segmentations. Laurel's *T* includes a quote from a piece by G. M. Tamás about "categories of people" who are considered non-citizens by the state, specifically one category and the reasoning behind it: "'*Homosexuals, by their inability or unwillingness to procreate, / bequeath and continue a living refutation of the alleged link / between nature and history.*'"[1] It seems clear, at least to me, that partly what is at stake in *T* is an interrogation of label and

1. Laurel Uziell, *T* (London: Materials, 2020), unpaginated. G. M. Tamás, 'What is Post-fascism?,' 13 September 2001.

identity or any funnelling of their dramatic playing out in life into box-ticking and form-filling. Laurel asks, implicitly, what can the T of LGBTQ hold? The 'Acknowledgements' rubbishes the notion that there can be a category such as 'trans writing' which could get neatly shelved away, thanking Nat Raha, Callie Gardner, and Verity Spott "for making 'trans writing' possible and showing it to be an utterly meaningless designation." I think for Laurel this is partly about having the work evade capture. As Tom Leonard points out: "possession is irretrievably bound up with categorization, and the function of the critic is to categorize, that the bourgeoisie might safely possess."[2]

Let's get to that again from another angle. In what sense might we consider Maggie O'Sullivan's *A Natural History in 3 Incomplete Parts* (1985) to be a work of *natural history?* In a broad sense, a natural history is not only a text which includes flora and fauna, but a history of processes taking place in accordance with or as a result of natural laws. What constitute *natural laws* is a fraught question. Human laws, customs, and history often confront individuals with the force of natural laws, so it is not always clear where natural laws end and culture begins. In Maggie's text, the juxtaposition of text about flora and newspaper articles powerfully torques the natural and human worlds together. I am thinking mainly of the collages in 'Moral Conditions' (a phrase with a thoroughly nineteenth century air to it), itself in 'More Incomplete.'[3] Calling attention to worldly things, letting the thing-we-normally-call-poetry recede, this is the most shocking gesture of the work – and it is certainly the part that accrues most commentary. Why do these newspaper articles intervene in, or rather rest on top of, the text – and on top of text we have already encountered, already read? Is it *natural* that, as one newspaper headline announces, a Royal Ulster Constabulary member should go "berserk"? Was the northern Irish conflict something David Attenborough could have narrated? Is it natural that the language appears as it does on the page, or that the newspaper headline appears on top of the pages in question? I think the drama of Maggie's work is that while on first encountering a page of poetry we think of it as first nature, the same page appears later covered over by something clearly of second nature, i.e. political events. Where we see first nature it is transmuted into second nature. And it keeps happening: "blood.

2. Tom Leonard, 'The Proof of the Mince Pie,' *Definite Articles: Selected Prose 1973-2012* (Devon: etruscan/Edinburgh: Word Power, 2013), pp. 91-99: p. 92.

3. Maggie O'Sullivan, *A natural history in 3 incomplete parts* (London: Magenta, 1985), unpaginated.

that.morning.dipping.slits. / darned.poppy.orange.realistic. / Oranger."[4] Is this a ramble through nature? I might initially think so, but "poppy" and "orange" in close recall poppies as mnemonic for a particular reading of WWI, a memorial frequently avoided or downplayed by Irish nationalists because a rebellion against colonial British rule began during WWI, and orange is a colour with Protestant and unionist associations through the Orange Order, a conservative unionist organisation based in occupied Northern Ireland.

One weekend in lockdown in early 2021 after it snowed I looked out the back garden and saw what looked like a gigantic wildcat bouncing around. It was the size of a house, a large doll's house, it was four to five times the size of our housecats, Ticklepenny and Worf. Excitedly, I called for Nisha to come and see. By the time she came, it was gone, and I wondered if it was real. But Nisha had been on the local forums, and reported with confidence that it was probably the much-maligned "monster cat," someone's eccentric pet. We are always encountering things as if they are first nature. Cats. Categories. There is a morphism or functor between these.

A painting by Frances Kruk, dated 22nd May 2008 and I'm pretty sure called *Black Glove*, adorns a wall on the room I looked out from. Her *Discourse on Vegetation & Motion* (2007), a Baconian natural history, contains similar moments of misrecognition. For example:

> today is 1646 & I rub Amber
> fiddle Genitals, spark for Electrolysis
> Thus I conjure
> some tasty Soldier for to test
> It is known I don't approve of War
> yet I bubble
> I violent
> I set out to broomrape
> every One[5]

It is 1646, the First English Civil War is playing out, or it is 14 minutes to 17:00, or something. In line 8, we get "broomrape," a genus of over 200 species of parasitic herbaceous plants mostly native to the temperate Northern

---

4. Maggie O'Sullivan, *Body of Work* (East Sussex: Reality Street, 2006), p. 75.
5. Frances Kruk, *A Discourse on Vegetation & Motion* (Cambridge: Critical Documents, 2012 [2008]), unpaginated.

Hemisphere. They completely lack chlorophyll, bearing yellow, white, or blue flowers. When not flowering, none of it is visible above the surface. It is totally dependent on other plants for nutrients. But, grammatically and in its setup ("I violent"), the plant's name is inescapably a verb – broom*rape*. Later in the book "Shidane Arone" is mentioned, a Somalian teenager who was brutally beaten and sodomoized with a broomstick in 1993 by Canadian soldiers participating in, ahem, humanitarian efforts in Somalia. Yes, you read that right. Again, flora slides into second nature or the realm of human action, or rather the reverse, second sliding to first. I imagine that the speaker is setting out to avenge Arone. Who is included in "every One"? And are there other victims in the text? Perhaps. Earlier in the text we read "today I am Ally Sheedy." The page alludes to *The Breakfast Club* (1985), but Ally Sheedy also played Detective Kelly Brooks in *Our Guys: Outrage at Glen Ridge* (1999). The film is based on an event in 1989, when a mentally disabled girl was raped with a broom by members of the Glen Ridge High School football team in New Jersey. The assailants were given special treatment by the school and local authorities due to their status as members of the local football team. The world where these events happened is right outside. It is inside too. The window doesn't matter. The "Window goes white in fear."[6]

At another point in the text, the poem mentions its "spoiled Plaints." A plaint is an audible expression of sorrow, the expression in verse or song of that sorrow. This is chiefly poetic after the 17th century. But it is also a statement or representation of wrong, injury, or injustice suffered – the plaintiff in a legal proceeding. What court is it that this poetry takes Arone's case to? I don't know, but I do know that poetry is not meant to function in this work as an idealized court nor as an area for wish-fulfilment of the same. It is not a merely compensatory space. It might be an exercise in its own jurisprudential fecundity, like the jurisprudence of a children's playground, in all its trouble and beauty. The 'Afterword' to Laurel's *T* discusses the main text as a kind of response to a court case:

> Between 2017-2018 I was involved in a trial with a group of
> TERFs after a scuffle emerged during a counter protest against
> a 'debate' about sex-based rights in light of proposed reforms
> to the Gender Recognition Act which would have made trans
> people's lives marginally easier. Luckily I wasn't actually in the

---

6. Kruk, *A Discourse on Vegetation & Motion*.

dock, but I appeared to give evidence, and for everyone involved it was a humiliating ordeal as we were doxxed, harassed online and in real life, while the relentless media campaign which ensued took a toll on the entire trans community. The caricaturesque reduction of a complex interrelation of political positions, epistemologies, traumas and personal grievances into two 'sides' ultimately worked to further the persecution of trans people, but nevertheless highlighted a social logic on whose terms the so called debate was forced to appear: sex was pitted against gender (or more revealingly 'gender identity'), objective biology against subjective 'self-identification', nature against culture, or, perhaps, first nature against second nature.

Nisha visited that trial briefly. I've never been in a courtroom. One of the epigraphs to Nisha's 'a basket woven of one's own hair' asks what musical "categorisation" is for. Dhanveer Singh Brar's essay on Dean Blunt's music and blackness in Britain asks: "Why does the categorisation of music function so similarly to the modes of categorisation used to racially determine the nation? Why does the free movement of music across the border of genre raise such violent consternation?"[7] Nisha's poem has the line: "Onomatopoeia is the containerisation of the past in the present (in the future); the valorisation of perfect rhyme at the expense of grain; the ratification of sameness in service of representation."[8] Onomatopoeia is when a word describes the sound, or *is* the sound. This kind of word pretends to be unmediated mimesis of the object – a plonk sounds like when you say plonk, right? Word and referent merge. But in another language, tick tock becomes katchin katchin. These words are not intuitive or natural, even if they are not wholly arbitrary. This is one way in which onomatopoeia is a container, it traps us inside something, our language, which we take to be natural. Another thing onomatopoeia does, the poem claims, is hold the "past in the present." It carries history. This might be the truth of onomatopoeia – it is true that through conditioning and encounters with a long and very real cultural history, we take this or that word to be a direct reference to a sound we really hear. We may even hear a plonk as a plonk. This,

7. Dhanveer Singh Brar, *Beefy's Tune (Dean Blunt edit)* (London: the87press, 2020), p. 23.
8. Nisha Ramayya, 'a basket woven of one's own hair,' *The Hythe*, 20th Aug. 2020.

the poem tells us via semicolon, is the valorization of perfect rhyme – rhyme between word and world – but it comes "at the expense of grain." Perhaps this grain is a sound-based grain rather than food, as grains are the small bits of a sound recording, and less granularity = less audio fidelity. This then ratifies ("ratification"), gives legal soundness, to sameness or homogeneity (perhaps from "past" to "present" and "future") in order to represent a thing. What this line asks of us, then, is to attempt to forget this "sameness," or work against its grain, in order to challenge orders of representation which, as the next line states, might have racialised undercurrents or problems – it attempts to undermine the prominence of onomatopoeia within a single language in favour of a multilingual decoupling, temporarily, of sound and referent – a decoupling onomatopoeia fantasizes it has overcome. This overcoming is a violent fantasy – Nisha was telling me ages ago about an artwork she saw at a gallery where she held a residency, called 'Conflicted Phonemes,' which highlighted the use of language analysis in determining the origin of asylum seekers and subsequently had their asylum claims rejected. A group organized by Lawrence Abu Hamdan produced it, including twelve Somalians who had all been subjected to a language, dialect, or accent analysis by Dutch immigration authorities and subsequently had their asylum requests rejected. A pseudoscientific analysis of their accents was trusted above their own testimony, it was considered more real than their real lives. The realm of second nature, of acquired accent through cultural interaction, was taken for first nature, geographical origin imagined as a point. As if sound can be directly mimetic of a person's history, like it can portray a plonk. The neat fold of form and content. All this by way of subcenograph. I have never read a literary critical PhD thesis or article which does not, at some point, gesture at how form and content speak each other, and even if not *that* the dehiscence and dissonance of form and content is shown to be performed by the text in some manner, which collapses into pretty much the same thing
doing exactly what they say on their tin
I don't want to meet where we are
on the ledger
    the ledge
it happens every day like a fucking zoom it happens all the time
but where we're not just not
the attorney or the barrister on zoom
it isn't *my* job and I didn't want any particular outcome

I didn't want to have to come here
or support your application for citizenship
in the reverse-colonization of pain
    it hates my answers
refusing to be under strain
in a mask in a zoo telling the judge he is not a cat
      like on the tin it
isn't *my* job it isn't *your* job putting
the label on the tin listen what
you hear is what you get what you ask for what
is it the fossil, the law as count before which operation nothing counts
an extinct instrumentation
like it had feelings or something
only we know how greedy we are for blood
set out set out to want
to meet where we're not just
    don't meet me where you are
but where we're not just what we do
but what we could do soon

## Long Winded

There was a time I thought I suffered.
who is it taught us
that suffering is private

Tom told me
everyone should have a large head wound
to improve politics.

I wanted to write a song interspersed with wallets.
I wanted to write about the trees but they kept wriggling and rustling

To count is to feel texture. To measure something you have to ask
it to lie down or stay still, place carefully amorphous units
of measurement on top until you can't see it.

it is hard to make films,
  harder to stop

# LAY OUT YOUR UNREST